Courtes
GWINNETT C
PUBLIC LIE

What is a food chain?

Bobbie Kalman

🌱 **Crabtree Publishing Company**
www.crabtreebooks.com

Created by Bobbie Kalman

Author and Editor-in-Chief
Bobbie Kalman

Educational consultants
Elaine Hurst
Joan King
Jennifer King

Notes for adults
Jennifer King

Editors
Kathy Middleton
Crystal Sikkens

Design
Bobbie Kalman
Katherine Berti

Photo research
Bobbie Kalman

Print and production coordinator
Katherine Berti

Prepress technician
Katherine Berti

Illustrations
Barbara Bedell: page 23

Photographs
Corel: page 15 (bottom)
Photos.com: page 5
Other photographs by Shutterstock

Library and Archives Canada Cataloguing in Publication

Kalman, Bobbie, 1947-
    What is a food chain? / Bobbie Kalman.

(My world)
Includes index.
Issued also in electronic format.
ISBN 978-0-7787-9567-4 (bound).--ISBN 978-0-7787-9592-6 (pbk.)

    1. Food chains (Ecology)--Juvenile literature. I. Title. II. Series:
My world (St. Catharines, Ont.)

QH541.14.K363 2011   j577'.16   C2010-907448-3

Library of Congress Cataloging-in-Publication Data

Kalman, Bobbie.
    What is a food chain? / Bobbie Kalman.
        p. cm. -- (My world)
    Includes index.
    ISBN 978-0-7787-9592-6 (pbk. : alk. paper) -- ISBN 978-0-7787-9567-4
(reinforced library binding : alk. paper) -- ISBN 978-1-4271-9674-3
(electronic (pdf))
    1. Food chains (Ecology)--Juvenile literature. I. Title. II. Series.

QH541.14.K354 2011
577'.16--dc22
                                                              2010047126

Crabtree Publishing Company

www.crabtreebooks.com   1-800-387-7650

Printed in China/022011/RG20101116

Published in Canada
Crabtree Publishing
616 Welland Ave.
St. Catharines, Ontario
L2M 5V6

Published in the United States
Crabtree Publishing
PMB 59051
350 Fifth Avenue, 59th Floor
New York, New York 10118

Published in the United Kingdom
Crabtree Publishing
Maritime House
Basin Road North, Hove
BN41 1WR

Published in Australia
Crabtree Publishing
386 Mt. Alexander Rd.
Ascot Vale (Melbourne)
VIC 3032

What is in this book?

Energy!

We are **living things**.
Plants and animals are
other living things.
Living things need air,
sunlight, and water
to stay alive.
Living things
also need **energy**.
Energy is the power
we need to move.
We cannot do anything
without energy!

Plants need energy to grow
and make new plants.
Animals need energy to move,
grow, find food, and stay safe.

We need food!

Food gives plants, animals, and people the energy they need. The energy in food comes from the sun.

This girl is standing in a **wheat** field.
She is holding bread made from wheat.
Wheat has energy from the sun.

wheat

wheat field

bread

7

It starts with plants

People and animals cannot use
the energy from sunlight to make food.
Only plants can make food
with the sun's energy.
Plants have a special green color
in their leaves, called **chlorophyll**.
Chlorophyll catches sunlight.

Chlorophyll
catches the
sun's energy.

9

What is that word?

Plants use sunlight to make food from air and water.
A very long word describes how plants make food from sunlight.
The word is **photosynthesis**.

Chlorophyll gives this leaf its green color.

A plant's leaves catch sunlight.

A plant's leaves take in air.

The leaves let out fresh air.

soil   water

There is water in soil.
Plants use sunlight, air, and water to make food.

11

Energy flows

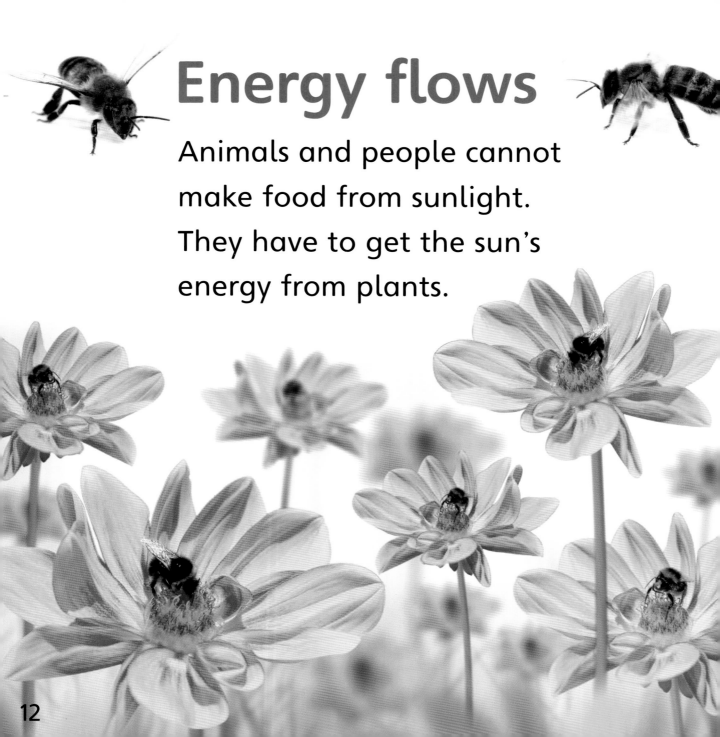

Animals and people cannot make food from sunlight. They have to get the sun's energy from plants.

When an animal eats a plant, the sun's energy flows from the plant to the animal.

When these bees eat the **nectar** in flowers, they are getting the energy of the sun. Nectar is a sweet liquid inside flowers.

energy

What is a herbivore?

A **herbivore** is an animal that eats plants.
Herbivores eat different kinds of plants.
Some also eat different parts of plants.
This squirrel is eating the seeds of a flower.
It is getting the sun's energy from the seeds.

sun

energy

energy

grass → energy → rabbit

The rabbit is eating grass.
The porcupine will eat these flowers.

flowers → energy → porcupine

What is a carnivore?

Some animals do not eat plants.
They eat other animals.
Animals that eat other animals
are called **carnivores**.

chameleon

The grasshopper is
eating a plant.
The chameleon will
eat the grasshopper.

spider

fly

The spider is going to eat the fly.
The snake is eating a frog.

frog

snake

17

What is a food chain?

A **food chain** is the passing of the sun's energy from one living thing to another. The food chain on page 19 starts with plants. Next, the energy goes into the rabbit that eats the plants. When the lynx eats the rabbit, the sun's energy is passed along to the lynx. The plants, rabbit, and lynx make up the food chain.

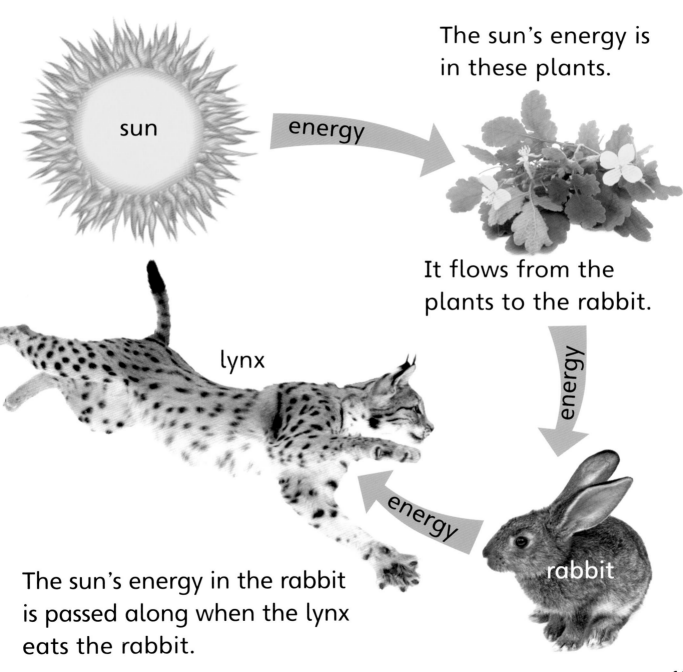

The sun's energy is in these plants.

energy

sun

It flows from the plants to the rabbit.

energy

lynx

energy

rabbit

The sun's energy in the rabbit is passed along when the lynx eats the rabbit.

A food web

Animals eat more than one
kind of food, just as you do.
When they eat different foods,
they belong to more than one food chain.
When two or more food chains are
in one place, there is a **food web**.
The food web on the next page
is in a forest.

Foxes eat squirrels and chipmunks.

Cougars eat squirrels and chipmunks.

Squirrels and chipmunks eat nuts and seeds.

Nuts and seeds contain the sun's energy.

What do they eat?

Some of these animals eat both plants and other animals. They are called **omnivores**. Guess which of these animals are omnivores.

skunk

chipmunk

raccoon

fox

bear

mouse

Answer

They are all omnivores!

22

Words to know and Index

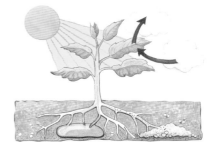

Notes for adults

Objectives
- to teach children about food chains and food webs
- to understand photosynthesis
- to teach children about energy

Before reading the book
Put the following words on the board or chart paper: plant, animal, living thing, human, and energy. Ask the children to give examples of each one.

Questions after reading
"What do plants, animals, and people have in common?" (We are living things.)
"What do living things need?" (air, sunlight, water, food)
"Where do living things get their energy?" (from the sun, plants, food)
"Where do plants get their energy?" (go through the steps of photosynthesis)
"How do animals and humans get energy?"(by eating food)
"How does energy flow?" (from the sun to plants to animals or people)
"What are herbivores?" (plant-eaters)
"Name three herbivores from the book." (rabbit, squirrel, porcupine)
"What are carnivores?" (animals that eat other animals)
"Name three carnivores from the book." (spider, chameleon, snake)
"What will the spider eat?" (fly)
"What will the chameleon eat?" (grasshopper)
"What is the snake eating?" (frog)
"What do we call two or more food chains?" (food web)

Activity: Felt-board food chain
Pre-cut the sun, plants, and various animals from felt. Have the children pin the pictures on a felt board in the order of a food chain. You can amplify this activity by using seeds and nuts, a squirrel and chipmunk, and a cougar and fox to make a food web. You can even extend the food web by adding the rabbit and lynx.

Extension
Introduce the *The habitats of baby animals series* by Bobbie Kalman to your children. The books are at **Guided reading levels K and L** and are filled with wonderful pictures of baby animals in forest, grassland, wetland, mountain, desert, and ocean habitats. The concepts in the books include habitats, life cycles, and food chains.

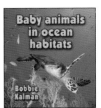

For teacher's guide, go to www.crabtreebooks.com/teachersguides